A BIRD CALLED ELAEUS

David Constantine was born in 1944 in Salford, Lancashire. He read Modern Languages at Wadham College, Oxford, and lectured in German at Durham from 1969 to 1981 and at Oxford from 1981 to 2000. He is a freelance writer and translator, a Fellow of the Queen's College, Oxford, and was co-editor of *Modern Poetry in Translation* from 2004 to 2013. He was awarded The Queen's Gold Medal for Poetry for 2020, presented to him by HM Queen Elizabeth in 2021. He lives in Oxford and on Scilly.

He has published eleven books of poetry, five translations and a novel with Bloodaxe. His poetry titles include *Something for the Ghosts* (2002), which was shortlisted for the Whitbread Poetry Award; *Collected Poems* (2004), a Poetry Book Society Recommendation; *Nine Fathom Deep* (2009), *Elder* (2014) and *Belongings* (2020). His Bloodaxe translations include editions of Henri Michaux and Philippe Jaccottet; his *Selected Poems* of Hölderlin, winner of the European Poetry Translation Prize, and his version of *Hölderlin's Sophocles*, combined in a new expanded Hölderlin edition, *Selected Poetry* (2018); his translation of Hans Magnus Enzensberger's *Lighter Than Air*, winner of the Corneliu M. Popescu Prize for European Poetry Translation; and *A Bird Called Elaeus: poems for here and now from The Greek Anthology* (2024). His other books include *A Living Language: Newcastle/Bloodaxe Poetry Lectures* (2004), his translation of Goethe's *Faust* in Penguin Classics (2005, 2009), his monograph, *Poetry* (2013), in Oxford University Press's series *The Literary Agenda*, and his co-translation (with Tom Kuhn) of *The Collected Poems of Bertolt Brecht* (W.W. Norton, 2018).

He has published six collections of short stories, and won the Frank O'Connor International Short Story Award in 2013 for his collection *Tea at the Midland* (Comma Press), and was the first English writer to win this prestigious international fiction award. Four other short story collections, *Under the Dam* (2005), *The Shieling* (2009), *In Another Country: Selected Stories* (2015) and *The Dressing-Up Box* (2019), and his second novel, *The Life-Writer* (2015), are published by Comma Press. His story 'Tea at the Midland' won the BBC National Short Story Award in 2010, while 'In Another Country' was adapted into *45 Years*, a major film starring Tom Courtenay and Charlotte Rampling.

A Bird Called *Elaeus*

poems for here and now from
The Greek Anthology

translated & arranged by
DAVID CONSTANTINE

BLOODAXE BOOKS

ISBN: 978 1 78037 722 3

First published 2024 by
Bloodaxe Books Ltd,
Eastburn,
South Park,
Hexham,
Northumberland NE46 1BS.

www.bloodaxebooks.com
For further information about Bloodaxe titles
please visit our website and join our mailing list
or write to the above address for a catalogue.

Supported using public funding by
**ARTS COUNCIL
ENGLAND**

Cover design: Neil Astley & Pamela Robertson-Pearce.

Printed in Great Britain by Bell & Bain Limited, Glasgow, Scotland, on
acid-free paper sourced from mills with FSC chain of custody certification.

For Helen

The Greek Anthology

An anthology is a 'gathering of flowers'. *The Greek Anthology*, marvellous salvage from the vast shipwreck of the Ancient World, is a collection of about 4500 poems composed over more than fifteen hundred years by about three hundred authors, a colossal continuity and variety from pre-classical times through Roman into Byzantine. Sappho is there at the outset, in the mid-sixth century BC.

The *Anthology* grew out of successive 'garlands', the first woven by Meleager in the first century BC. Three more such composers can be named; and parts of their collections, together with parts of others whose composers are unknown, were, perhaps in the early tenth century, incorporated into and arranged in the fifteen books now preserved in a single manuscript in the Palatine Library in Heidelberg. In the fourteenth century that grand collection was meddled with by a monk called Maximus Planudes. He cast out poems which he found offensive but added others, which without his interference would have been lost, on statues and works of art. Loeb publishes these as an appendix, Book XVI. All the original garlands are lost. The surviving sixteen books are only a small portion of a superabundance of treasured Greek poetry at one time or another gathered in.

My preoccupation with *The Greek Anthology* began in 1975. By then, because of my work on Hölderlin, the Ancient World had become vitally important to me; and access to it, increased knowledge of it, was closest to hand in its literature. I read more in *The Anthology* in the early 1980s, because of Brecht. In July 1940, during their exile in Finland, Brecht's son Stefan gave him a selection of the poems translated into German by August Oehler and published in 1920. Brecht admired in them what he called their *Gegenständlichkeit*: that is, their grasp and depiction of the so-ness, the exact reality, of things. The encounter was of great importance in his endeavour at the time to (as he put it) 'wash the language clean', so that it would serve truth in the struggle against Hitler's lies. He wanted clarity, grace and beauty on his side too, and discerned them through Oehler's translations in the Greek. We can study Brecht's most successful practice of such language in his *War Primer*, the book of photographs with poem-captions he began compiling in exile but could not publish till 1955, a year before his death. The following quatrain, here in my translation, stands below four photos of afflicted children (Greek, Russian, Sicilian and French) and is, as it were, spoken by them:

> You in your tanks and bombers, warriors
> Sweating in Algiers, freezing in Lapland's ice
> Coming from a hundred battles as conquerors:
> We are the ones you conquered. Oh rejoice!

Hölderlin and Brecht: poets as soon as I met them I knew I could not do without. Translating them has helped me with my English. In German there's a deep etymological association between the words 'denken' – to think – and 'danken' – to thank. 'Andenken' is 'a thinking of gratefully'. There's a similar connection in Old English. The noun 'thank' meant 'a grateful thought, gratitude'. That kind of thinking is a prime mover in Hölderlin's poetry. But remembering such debts of gratitude is altogether very salutary. It keeps the dead, and not only the poets among them, alive and active in us. They help us live.

So various these garlands of poetry are, so tangible and of such lived life. Leafing through their inexhaustible plenty, I've settled very often not just on the love poems but also on the many that commemorate the beloved dead (humans and animals) and those that are dedications of useful and valued objects – a lyre, a caul, a creel, for example – or of placatory gifts, to one deity or another. And during my latest bout of benign obsession, beginning in lockdown in the Year

8

of the Plague 2020 and continuing (as the Plague has) still, I've gone to poems that treat man's dealings with the natural world, his work and trades there, the creatures other than himself who inhabit it and the divinities whose care it is. Lockdown, amidst all the sickness and dying, gave lucky people the experience of something akin to idyll: the quietened roads and skies, the audible birdsong and an extraordinary flowering and fruiting in the gardens. As though Gaia were showing us what we risk forfeiting for ever. I translated poems that felt like a reinforcement of her final warning. The Ancient World was not populated by humans harmless to the earth, not at all: often they, like us, did the worst their means enabled them to do. Still there were laws. *These things you must not do.* Doing them nevertheless was understood as transgression of laws beyond the human laws. You offended Demeter at your peril. Understand that how we like, it's the same now. And the peril is infinitely greater, threatens to be final, consuming the innocent with the guilty. Good poems live in a present tense and many in *The Greek Anthology* address our situation here and now.

I say I translated these poems, and I must explain briefly what I mean by that. Working on Hölderlin it became necessary for me to understand what he was seeking in his highly idiosyncratic translations of the sixth-century poet Pindar's 'Victory Odes'. He cleaved exactly to the foreign text, its word-order, its line-breaks, word-for-word literal and often going for the root, not the most usual, sense. And by this procedure he arrived at a German scarcely intelligible but instructive to him who was, in practice, learning his own language again, to do things with it no German poet had done before. My own procedure was a mild version of his. I should have gone to classes, but didn't. I got my Greek from teach-yourself books, dictionaries, cribs and from copying out page upon page of the lovely ancient script. Half a century of that and I still wouldn't pass GCSE. With the *Anthology*, I read the quaint translations (by W.R. Paton), moved from them to the facing originals and with an idiot patience and labour and my massive and beloved Liddell & Scott worked out an exactly word-for-word literal version. Then began to cast that into verse of my own.

The vast majority of the poems in the *Anthology* are composed in elegiac couplets – that is, hexameter + pentameter, six feet + five feet. Most translators into a language which scans not by length of syllable, as the Greek does, but by stress (English, German), have gone for rhyming pentameters, as Brecht does in the quatrain I quoted above. Rhyming was one of my options, a variety of schemes and line-lengths, and the rhymes might be pure or half or even less than half. But I also used strictly syllabic lines (deciding on a number of syllables and sticking to it) or loosely imitated the Greek hexameter-pentameter couplets. For this present collection – my small anthology of the vast original – I have quite often taken the liberty of bringing already urgent poems closer to home and our accelerating drift towards the Sixth Extinction. Several times I expanded a Greek text, once or twice combined two poems into one or wrote a poem of my own for a particularly telling context. But most often I kept close, doing my level best to bring into my English what was so *livingly* there in the Greek.

I have translated much of the work the *Anthology* contains by women poets: that is, by Sappho, 2; by Anyte of Tegea, 20 or 21; by Nossis, 3 or 4 (one attribution in either case is uncertain); and by Moero of Byzantium, 2. Of Erinna's three I have translated one of a pair concerning the death of her friend Baucis; and in addition two by men praising her work and lamenting her very early death. Altogether precious little poetry by women has survived let alone had its due. (Josephine Balmer's *Classical Women Poets*, Bloodaxe Books, 1996, does the few a great service.)

The ordering of the poems in this small selection from

the *Greek Anthology*'s thousands is not according to author, volume, book, date or topic. And though in poem after poem many stories are told, the thing in its entirety is more kaleidoscope than narrative. I hoped that strategy would be productive of insights and connexions in the reader. Other arrangements, giving other slants and emphases, would of course be possible. The whole is divided into five parts, each of which has its particular but not exclusive concerns. The general direction of travel is towards the state we are in now.

The poems are given a location first by volume and number in the *Greek Anthology* itself, then by volume and page in the Loeb edition. All five volumes are still in print and can also be read and studied in that edition gratis online at several sites, *The Online Books Page* being one. Liddell & Scott's *Greek-English Lexicon* is similarly accessible. Wikipedia has a good article on the *Anthology* and brief biographical notes on at least some of the poets.

ACKNOWLEDGEMENTS

My thanks are due to the editors of the following publications in which some of these poem-translations first appeared: Bloodaxe Books, *Bracken*, *Dymock Poets and Friends*, Liveright Publishing Corporation, *Modern Poetry in Translation*, *Poems on the Underground*, *Poetry Salzburg*, University of Swansea *Festschrift*.

I

GA X, no. 3; Loeb IV, p. 4
Anonymous

The way to Hades is straight down. You leave from here
Or cross an ocean to an elsewhere, never fear
Wherever you arrive it is a place of departure.
A wind sets fair for Hades from every quarter.

GA IX, no. 683; Loeb III, p. 380
Anonymous

Arethusa the woman, Alpheus the man
Eros mixed their waters and married them.
Henceforth wherever they ran
Fast or meandering, deep or shallow
He tasted of her, she of him
Contributed to, sucked up, let go
As rain or snow, sweet into the sea
They became a current of she and he
In drought, as dust, as seeds in the air
Dormant they dreamed that once they were
Two springs on separate hills until
Love mingled them and since then
He tastes of woman and she of man
And both of both and they always will.

GA V, no. 155; Loeb I, p. 202
Meleager

Dreaming, Love whispered to me she was real.
Waking, I felt her in my very heart and soul.

15

GA IX, no. 144; Loeb III, p. 74
Anyte of Tegea

Here Cypris stands for she is pleased to be
On land a watcher of the shining sea
And helper of those who sail it. From her bright face,
Wherever she turns, the light shivers the surface.

GA IX, no. 333; Loeb III, p. 180
Mnasalcas

When let they will go again and watch till the falling tide
Allows them to paddle down that long low spit of land
As far as the sanctuary of Cypris of the Sea
And halt like children there in silence hand in hand
And watch the kingfishers flitting to the lip of her well
Whose waters through the salt rise sweet and plentiful
Into the shadow of the whispering black poplar tree.
So they will watch the quick birds drink in the time allowed.

GA XVI, no. 276; Loeb V, p. 324
Bianor
On a statue of Arion

Periander set up the statue of Arion on this shore
And of the dolphin who swam him to safety here
When he was in peril. My fellow humans, says Arion
Would have murdered me. A fish was my salvation.

GA IX, no. 332; Loeb III, p. 180
Nossis

That day she showed me in the temple by the sea
The wooden and gold-leafed statue of Aphrodite
And said: Polyarchis set it here to be
Her thanks for the given riches of her body.

GA VII, no. 291; Loeb II, p. 158
Xenocritus of Rhodes

The salt sea combs your flowing hair, Lysidice.
It cast you from the tilting ship like a leaded seine
And you sank fast. You will beach alone
On a cold shore somewhere stripped to the bone.
Your father Nicanor escorted you safe
Neither to your new home as the awaited wife
Nor to the old as corpse. This tomb holds only grief
But tells your land, Cyme, and name, Lysidice.

GA VI, no. 211; Loeb I, p. 408
Leonidas of Tarentum

The bangle from around her ankle, her silver Eros
Her breast band the faint-blue colour of glass
The broad boxwood comb that gathered her rich hair
The purple caul, the bronze mirror, all this
Now having attained her heart's desire
Does Calliclea of Lesbos
Lay down in the porch of the one true Cypris.

GA VI, no. 273; Loeb I, p. 444
After Nossis

Artemis, lady of Delos and of lovely Ortygia
Lay down your bright bow in the lap of the Graces
Cleanse your body in the Inopus and come to Locri
And from the hard pangs of childbirth deliver Alcetis.

GA VI, no. 270; Loeb I, p. 444
Nicias

The headscarf and the watery-blue veil of Amphareta
Now, as she promised, are yours to wear, Eileithyia
For you did as she prayed you would in her childbed labour
And kept the goddesses of death away from her.

GA VI, no. 202; Loeb I, p. 402
Leonidas of Tarentum

At your virginal doors, o Artemis, daughter of Leto
I, Athis, hang my dress and my prettily netted zone
Now you from my labour have eased me and let go
Out of my lightened womb a living child of my own.

GA VII, no. 190; Loeb II, p. 108

Anyte of Tegea (*or* Leonidas of Tarentum)

For her cicada, singer in the cool leaves of the oaks
And her cricket, singer in the noon sun in the fields
Myro has made one tomb. What Hades takes
No tears will ever bring back, not even a child's.

GA VII, no. 166; Loeb II, p. 94

Dioscorides *or* Nicarchus

Here lies concealed on the banks of the Libyan Nile
Lamisca, child of Nicarete and Eupolis
Of Samos, with her twin babies, stillborn in such pains
They killed her. She was twenty. Come now, unmarried girls
Bearing the gifts that belong to childbed and pour
The libation of your warm tears over her cold tomb.

GA VII, no. 299; Loeb II, p. 162

Nicomachus

This was our city. Beyond belief but true:
The sky fell on it and it fell on us.
Left among the living then were very few.
Over the very many lay this tumulus.

GA VII, no. 298; Loeb II, p. 162
Anonymous

Two joined that day, under one roof that night
Lying in the wedlock darkness had begun to see
How much their lips and hands could bring to light
How slow and lovely long their learning curve would be.

GA VII, no. 375; Loeb II, p. 200
Antiphilus of Byzantium

They cite the woman who found herself confined
In her own inner room that smelled of underground
Timbers and lintels falling in such a way
They left a breathing space and there she lay

And saw a hole above and daylight coming through
Then only darkness with a star or two
Staring at which, she felt her pains begin
Sure she would die, and saw day come again

And fetched her baby out and heard him cry
And bit the cord and saw that very high
Bright things were crossing with a swallow grace
And pale streamers, on blue. And then a down-turned face.

She could not speak, her baby cried. Ladder
Stretcher, ropes, they fetched both out of there.
Rescue of a mother and child from underground.
Just one such outcome proves the gods are kind.

GA IX, no. 89; Loeb III, p. 46
Philippus of Thessalonica

Old woman, hungering, to earn a bite to eat
Gleaning with the girls she dropped dead in the heat.
Grieving, praying for a better end, of the stalks stripped bare
They built their fellow-worker a funeral pyre.
Mother Demeter, take no offence: of what she could not eat
Earth's children built a hungry woman a consuming fire.

GA VII, no. 490; Loeb II, p. 266
Anyte of Tegea

I weep for the girl Antibia, she whose beauty and prudence
    Called to her father's house many an eager young man
Wanting marriage. Accursed Moira however
    Scattered their hopes like dust down the travelled roads.

GA VII, no. 173; Loeb II, p. 98
Diotimus *or* Leonidas of Tarentum

In the late afternoon the cattle came home to the byre
By themselves, from the hill, in heavily falling snow.
Therimachus, herdsman, felled by a stroke of fire
Lies under the oak on earth too warm for the drifting snow.

GA IX, no. 20; Loeb III, p. 12
Anonymous

I, formerly crowned winner on the Alpheus
Twice also at Delphi, by Castalia's cold springs
Once at Nemea and once, as a colt, on the Isthmus
I, a runner then with the wind's own wings
See me now in old age, sir, me whom they crowned
Driven, demeaned, shoving a millstone round and round.

GA VI, no. 168; Loeb I, p. 384
Paulus Silentiarius

He trampled the wavy tresses of our reeds into the mud
With his sharp tusks he grubbed up our kale and garlic
In our old vineyards and tender orchards he played havoc,
He devoured much and soiled still more of our livelihood
The sheep-dogs fled him but when I, Xenophilus
Encountered the boar by the sunny river
He had just come out of the wood's deep cover
It was my first close sight of the creature harming us
He halted, he raised his bristling great head at me
Bowed it and charged, I stood my ground, I ran him through
With this good bronze. Now, Pan, for you
I nail his rough hide on this graceful beech tree.

GA VII, no. 665; Loeb II, p. 354
Leonidas of Tarentum

Of what Promachus knew all along – no ship is safe
No matter her depth or length – came proof
When one gust of wind snapped off his mast and he was
      taken down
By one wave into a trough. Still, worse happens by far.
Yes, the corpse of this young man tumbled ashore
At home and he got what we all pray for and many in vain:
Burial in our native earth, love shown as the grief
Of dear ones in a lasting place, a sort of after-life.

GA IX, no. 564; Loeb III, p. 312
Nicias

Quick bee, the sweetly blossoming spring's discoverer
Yellow bee frenzied in this climax of things in flower
Whizz to my scented meadow now and get busy there
And cram your wax chambers full to the running over.

GA VI, no. 221; Loeb I, p. 414
Leonidas of Tarentum

That wintry night through driving hail, fleeing the snow
And the killing cold, a solitary lion, stricken
In all its limbs, entered the fold of goatherds who go
Surefootedly across sheer faces. They then
Ceased caring about their herd and sought salvation
By Zeus for themselves instead. But the lion
Beast of the night, done in, head on his paws, lay
Only waiting out the weather and at break of day
And harming not one of the goats or frightened men
Limped from the fold. The glad humans drew
A telling picture of what they had come through
On this oak's good trunk, for the mountaineer, Pan.

GA VII, no. 509; Loeb II, p. 276
Simonides

This tomb his friends raised over Cynyras in grief
And being glad of him and grateful for his life.

GA VI, no. 312; Loeb I, p. 468
Anyte of Tegea

The children fitted a crimson bridle round Goat's head
And taking turns raced him along the colonnade.
The god smiled. They are happy. So am I, Goat said
Not being slit from ear to ear and disembowelled and flayed.

GA IX, no. 412; Loeb III, p. 228
Philodemus

It is already the season of the rose, Sosylus
Of little fishes, the first-cut kale, the ripe chick-peas
The tender leaves of curly lettuces, fresh salted cheese.
It is the season of company and picnics, Sosylus
But we shall not go out on the headland to Cypris' garden
Chill the wine in her spring and talk and watch the boats
      come in
For we want the pair who yesterday were half our lives
And whom today we must carry to their graves.

GA V, no. 144; Loeb I, p. 196
Meleager

Already the white violets are in flower and the narcissi
That love the rain and on the hard dry mountain
The lilies have risen. And she herself, sweet Persuasion
Beckons me into the meadow where the playful breeze
Is lifting the grasses like unfastened hair. She says
They have said we are welcome here, you and I.

GA VII, no. 208; Loeb II, p. 118
Anyte of Tegea

Damis made this tomb for the brave warhorse he rode
Full into Ares, the impaler. That day were killed
Many men, many innocent horses. Their blood flowed
Into mouths of the earth whose thirst will not be stilled.

GA VI, no. 131; Loeb I, p. 368
Leonidas of Tarentum

These double-pointed spears, large shields and bridles in a row
Are subject and hang here to Pallas. Missing are
The horses and the men, their masters. The gear
Outlasts them who were softly made and have gone below.

GA V, no. 147; Loeb I, p. 198
Meleager

Into the myrtle, the white violets, the narcissi
I'll mingle scarlet hyacinths and purple crocuses and ply
Among smiling lilies the blood-red roses that are
What lovers crave. All this, Heliodora, for your crown.
I want to see and smell the sweet quarrel between
My manufacture and your unfastened scented hair.

GA VI, no. 266; Loeb I, p. 442
Hegesippus

This Artemis, Hagelochia, a king's daughter
Set here where three roads meet because to her,
Still a virgin in her father's house, the goddess came
Through the warp of her loom like a sheet of flame.

GA IX, no. 404; Loeb III, p. 222
Antiphilus of Byzantium

Lovely the juice the bees make under the infinite ether
And the hive, cosy tholos, all their sole manufacture
A gift freely given to the lives of humans, no call
For mattocks, curved sickles, oxen, just their small
Busy selves, in the murmuring home they let flow
Springs of sweetness abounding. Innocent creatures
Workers of the clear blue air, I salute you, go now
Pasture this early summer on unending flowers.

GA VII, no. 652; Loeb II, p. 348
Leonidas of Tarentum

The high sea turning savage lifted Agathon
And showed the empty sky the life he led:
This man, his little ship, his scant cargo
How slight an offering they were.
He lies now breathless with other carrion
Pickings for black-backs on a nameless shore.
Daily his mother Menippe, his father Aristo
Visit our headland polis of the missing dead
With offerings of fresh salt tears for their one son.

GA VI, no. 117; Loeb I, p. 362
Pancrates

His hammer, pliers and tongs Polycrates
Dedicates to you, Hephaestus.
Worker at the fire and the anvil all his days
He beat off poverty and won his children happiness.

GA VI, no. 123; Loeb I, 364
Anyte of Tegea

Stand there, spear of the ash tree's wood.
I do not wish to see, killer of men
Foully from your bronze point the blood
Of enemies dripping ever again.
Here in this house of light, in bright Athena's
Soaring temple bide now and proclaim
The manly virtue, victories and name
Of Cretan Echecratidas.

GA VI, no. 275; Loeb I, p. 446
Nossis

Symaetha offering you this caul that bound her hair
Thinks it will please you, Aphrodite. For it is
Delicately fashioned and smells still of the nectar
She anointed her lover with as you do your Adonis.

GA VI, no. 204; Loeb I, p. 404
Leonidas of Tarentum

Theris with gifted hands now giving up his trade
Dedicates to Pallas his cubit-rule, bright plane and axe
His saw with the worn curved grip and steady blade
His drill that turned up lovely shavings in a helix.

GA VI, no. 118; Loeb I, p. 362
Antipater (of Sidon or Thessalonica)

Three friends here dedicate to Phoebus Apollo
The implements of their chosen profession:
Phila, musician, her lyre; Sosis, archer, his horn bow;
Polycrates, hunter, his intricate net. Each one
For all prays to excel in what they do.

GA VII, no. 489; Loeb II, p. 266
Sappho

Timas approaching her wedding day has come to dust.
She drifts as a wraith in the house of Persephone now.
We, her companions, same age as her, for her we must
Razor our hair our lovers loved and ran their fingers through.

GA VII, no. 501; Loeb II, p. 272
Perses

Cold East Wind and the breakers have flung ashore
On Lesbos rich in wine, up under her sheer
Cliffs, a naked man. Between the unmoving stone
And the moving waters he will soon break down.

GA VII, np. 365; Loeb II, p. 194
Zonas of Sardis, also called Diodorus

Dour ferryman, coming for the child Euphorion
When you hush your prow through the reeds and touch the shore
Be kind. His father, standing in the muddy shallows
Will hand him up the plank. Reach down, Charon
Bring him carefully on board. Those are his first sandals
His pride and joy. But his footing in them is still unsure.

II

GA 10, no. 1; Loeb IV, p. 2
Leonidas of Tarentum

The season of sailing is here. The chattering swallows
Have returned. After the winds in uproar
Now by Zephyrus the sea is quietened. The meadows
Of Persephone are in flower. Mariner, weigh anchor
Loose the cables, set every stitch of sail. Priapus
God of the harbour, commands you. Now is
The time to learn how they have fared on the far shores
Time to exchange your news and your goods for theirs.

GA V, no. 201; Loeb I, 226
Anonymous

That night, all night, how busy we were.
I was learning to play his body and he mine.
So we gave and received till the rising of the morning star.
Grateful, we hang this lyre in Cypris' shrine.

GA VI, no. 176; Loeb I, p. 388
Macedonius the Consul

My dog, my barbed spear and my bag
I dedicate to Pan and the Dryads. But my dog
I'll take back living home again with me
To share what bit I have to eat and keep me company.

GA VI, no. 174; Loeb I, p. 388
Antipater (of Sidon or Thessalonica)

To Pallas these three girls all of an age and delicate
As the spider at weaving here have dedicated:
Demo her well-plaited workbasket
Arsinoe her spindle, worker of the well-spun thread
And Bacchylis the comb with which like a lyre-player
She plucked apart the warp to pass the shuttle through.
For each of them by the work of their hands, stranger
Desired to make a life that no flaw would undo.

GA VI, no. 226; Loeb I, p. 418
Leonidas of Tarentum

This here is Clito's bit of a dwelling, this
The bit of land he sows, that there's
His vineyard, that his wood, both scant. Nevertheless
Among these meagre ownings Clito's clocked up eighty years.

GA VI, no. 9; Loeb I, p. 302
Mnasalcas

The crooked bow and quiver from which were
Dispatched so many arrows of death, o Phoebus
Together they are hung up for you here
As votive offerings from Promachus.
But the arrows he cannot offer you since they
Bringers of terror in the battle's bloody mêlée
Lodge in the hearts of many men and pay
Thus with death for that hospitality.

GA VI, no. 265; Loeb I, p. 440
Nossis

Revered Hera Lacinia, come from your home in heaven
And in your earthly scented shrine accept this garment of linen
Woven for you by Cleocha's daughter, Theophilis
And her own dear radiant daughter, Nossis.

GA VI, no. 334; Loeb I, p. 476
Leonidas of Tarentum

Nymphs of the caves, the sacred hill and the clear water
That issues below in springs in the shade of the single pine
And you, Hermes, son of Maia, there watching over the sheep
And you, Pan, lord of the heights where the goats pasture
Accept these cakes of honey and barley and this full can of wine.
Crethon offers them, a poor farmer with a family to keep.

GA VII, no. 321; Loeb II, p. 172
Anonymous
Prayer for Amyntichus

Mother Earth, remembering how he laboured for you
Take the old man Amyntichus into your lap. He planted
Many ever-leafing olives in you and with the vines
Of Bacchus made you splendid. For your thirst and for
The music he channelled clear water over you, he raised
Your oats and barley, pot-herbs, the figs, the apples
The luscious peaches so that you would look your best
Under the sun and the heavens would pause over you

In delighted contemplation. So for his skills and courtesies
Beloved Earth, lie now gently on him who never stamped
Or marched on you, never burdened you with sloth nor
Disfigured you for lucre but loved the curving line
And honoured the contours, cover this local man sweetly
And wreathe in spring his grey head with your flowers.

GA XVI, no. 86; Loeb V, p. 204
Anonymous

Beware of the guardian of the kitchen garden, I
Am Priapus and, as you see, equipped. Best walk on by.
A poor man carved me out of fig wood with his old jack knife
No measuring, no polishing, but he got me to the life.
Laugh if you like, but touch his onions or his curly kale,
Girl or boy, man or woman, I promise you I'll have your tail.

GA VII, no. 13; Loeb II, p. 10
Leonidas of Tarentum *or* Meleager

Erinna a new voice in the poets' choir
Fresh gatherer of the honey of the Muses' flowers
She said to Death when he forced himself on her:
No life, no love of your own, you envy mortals theirs.

GA VII, no. 11; Loeb, II, p. 8
Asclepiades

This book holds all Erinna wrote. Not much but more
Of truth in it than many leave whose years by far
Exceed her scant nineteen. Death came for her too soon
And showed us what she was and would have been.

GA VII, 267; Loeb II, p. 146
Posidippus

Sailors, why must you bury me so near the sea?
Further off's the place for a shipwrecked man's poor tomb.
I shudder at the din of the waves that did for me.
But for your good intentions I wish you well all the same.

GA VII, no. 142; Loeb II, p. 80
Anonymous

This is the tomb of Achilles, breaker of the ranks of men.
We, the Achaeans, built it to haunt the Trojans now and for
     evermore.
We built it into the slope of the beach so that he may hear
Day and night Thetis grieving for her dead son.

GA VII, no. 142 a; Loeb II, p. 80
Anonymous

We buried Pylius, our comrade-in-hardship, here.
He sought a living, as we do, fishing and died dirt-poor.
We dug him as best we could into the slope of the shore
Close to the sea he frequented in love and fear.

GA VII, no. 656; Loeb II, p. 350
Leonidas of Tarentum

Traveller, salute the paltry mound and monument
Of lamentable Alcimenes hidden though it be
Under sharp thorns and brambles. My life was spent
Warring against them and now they have buried me.

GA VI, no. 79; Loeb I, p. 342
Agathias Scholasticus

Pan of the hills, to you the husbandman Stratonicus
Dedicates this unsown precinct in thanks for your kindness.
Feed your flocks, he says, and welcome. This plot, yours now
Never again will be furrowed by the plough.
Your new holding will be auspicious. Let grow
What will, let birds in many voices sing. Echo
Will be charmed here and do what you want her to do.
In Gaia's own grateful garden she will marry you.

GA VII, no. 539; Loeb II, p. 290
Perses

You set out on a cold voyage, Pelagon
Paid no heed to the evil setting of rainy Arcturus
But rowed with comrades in a many-oared ship
Across the Aegean fast into Hades. Daily here
Your mother, Calliope, your father, Diocles
Visit the vacant tomb they have built for you.

GA VI, no. 31; Loeb I, p. 314
Nicarchus?

Pan, mounter of many goats, and you fruitful Dionysus
And you, goddess of our earth, Mother Demeter, for this
One gift to you all, grant me a good herd, good wine
And from the ears of my small field plenteous good grain.

GA VII, no. 461; Loeb II, p. 250
Meleager

Mother Earth, on one who all his days
Never burdened you, lie lightly now upon Aisigenes.

GA VI, no. 2; Loeb I, p. 298
Simonides

This bow, retired from pitiless war and now slung here
Under the roof of Athena's temple, its arrows were
Dispatched through the dense thicket of the fight
And entered men and lodged and bled them white.

GA VI, no. 36; Loeb I, p. 316
Philippus of Thessalonica

To you, Demeter, mother of the harvest, Sosiscles, labourer,
Offers these fists of corn from the furrows of his small field.
A year of plenty. But grant that also next year
Often he must whet his sickle, so great the yield.

GA VI, no. 37; Loeb I, p. 316
Anonymous

We who pasture our herds on the mountains set here
At the windy crossroads to amuse you, Pan
This bough of an oak misshapen like an old man.
He begs you, have them, beasts and their minders, in your care.

GA IX, no. 334; Loeb III, p. 180
Perses

Me also, if you, labourer, at the right time, ask me
Small among the smaller gods, for nothing big, I guarantee
I'll do my best. I, Tychon, am a god who gives what he can:
Small things, common things, to the common man.

GA IX, no. 335; Loeb III, p. 180
Leonidas of Tarentum

Traveller, these two statues were given by Miccalion.
And you, Hermes, see how this worthy lugger of wood
Has managed in his miserable occupation
To be a giver of gifts. The good man is in all things good.

GA VI, no. 98; Loeb I, p. 350
Zonas

To Demeter the Winnower and to the Seasons who tread
To and fro in the furrows Heronax with little to till
Sets a share of the corn from his threshing-floor
And a few assorted pulses on this marble tripod.
His allotment being a scrap on the bad side of the hill
From its small yield he cannot offer you more.

GA VI, no. 42; Loeb I, p. 320
Anonymous

Having tasted the fruits of this abundant summer
Alcimenes from his small garden gives to Pan
One fig, one apple and a sup of cold water
From the spring below your rock. Being a poor man
He asks you, giver of the good things of life and the garden
That for what you receive you will return him more.

GA VII, no. 657; Loeb II, p. 350
Leonidas of Tarentum

Shepherds who traverse the beloved mountain, leading
Your fleecy sheep to slopes and hollows of good pasture
I, Cleitagoras, dead now, ask you in the name of
Mother Earth and of the lost daughter Persephone
This kindness: bring the flock to graze sometimes in earshot
So I may hear them bleating, and from Pan's hillock while

They get nourishment one of you breathe me the old tunes
And believe I listen and of any villager
Remembering me ask a garland of narcissi
To brighten my sepulchre and hold over that place
A ewe, the mother of pretty lambs, and let milk gush
From her udders on that wreath like needed rain. So will

I in the dark and you still in the sunlight hold fast
To one another for a while and your kindnesses
Will reach down like roots after moisture into the dark
And the thanks will be the seeding, the rush of blossom
Dewfall, birdsong for the ascent of Persephone.

GA VI, no. 21; Loeb I, p. 308
Anonymous

My fork, digger of the earth that is always thirsty
　My whetted sickle for cutting cabbages
My ragged cloak that kept the hard rain off my back
　My old rawhide boots that were comfortable
The dibble I prodded holes with in the giving earth
　For plants whose time had come to face the weather
And the hoe with which all the parched summer I guided
　Water along channels to every bed:
These things and my work in the garden outlasting me
　I, Philemon, dedicate to Priapus.

GA VII, no. 538; Loeb II, p. 288
Anyte of Tegea

Alive this Manes was a slave but is
Dead as powerful as great Darius.

GA VII, no. 651; Loeb II, p. 348
Euphorion

This earth of home does not contain you, Polymedes.
What of you still remains the indifferent sea
Mashes and grinds on the shingle of Icaria.
Here Phileas has shaped a vacant sepulchre
And set a stone lettered in blue that says
I bear the love of both of us in me.

GA VII, no. 180; Loeb II, p. 102
Apollonides

Death has moved on, master. The spacious grave
You should have occupied, I have, your slave.
Sent underground, building poor you a second home
The dome of it fell in and buried me.
Hades is not so bad as it is said to be.
All shades under this wan sun look much the same.

GA VI, no. 22; Loeb I, p. 308
Anonymous

A plum, softly bloomed, a pomegranate cracking open
    A fig with a wrinkled skin, its navel-stalk still adhering
A cluster of purple grapes, very tight and near bursting with juice
    And a filbert this minute stripped of its pale green ruffle:
These fruits of wood-stock and branch, I, their guardian, offer
    To sylvan Priapus, carved from one living trunk.

GA VII, no. 305; Loeb II, p. 166
Addaeus of Mitylene
Diotimus the fisherman

In the boat he fished from, getting a poor livelihood
At sunset, beaching, he housed in its stink and tackle
And when his time was up and he sank into the sleep
From which there is no awakening in that same boat
He rowed himself across to the dwellings of Hades.

The dead stood and watched him approaching with steady strokes
In a vessel of fire. The penniless fisherman
Who had done small harm to the lovely face of the earth
Pulled in the rhythm of a lifetime to the far shore
And lit black Acheron with a wake of dancing flames.

GA IX, no. 143; Loeb III, p. 74
Antipater of Sidon

Knowing your likings we have enthroned you here
In a simple house on a bar of sand near as we dare
To the breakers, in the very din of them. For this
Goddess of the wide and fickle sea watch over us
Bid the winds remember how easily we drown
Fetch us home from the grey-blue waters safe and sound
With our scant livings. Lady of the Shore, hearten
The wives, the mothers, the widows watching us in.

GA IX, no. 675; Loeb III, p. 376

Anonymous

The Lighthouse at Smyrna

Come in from the open sea without fear now
Make for my light in the darkness, mariners, make for harbour.
And you, the lost, native or foreign, by that light, you also
Head for safety, come back among people, come ashore.
And thank the Asclepiadae. I am their gift, they know
Grief for the drowned is a sickness hard to cure.

GA VII, no. 350; Loeb II, p. 188

Anonymous

Sailor, don't ask who in this cold tomb lies.
Ask only that you meet with kinder seas.

GA VII, no. 584; Loeb II, p. 312

Julianus, Prefect of Egypt

Salvaging me from the sea, housing me in the earth
Seafarer yourself, fare well. Give Malea a wide berth.
And may Luck be your lover but if she turns untrue
May you meet with such kindness as I had from you.

GA VII, no. 508; Loeb II, p. 276
Simonides

Gela, his city, buries Pausanias who did
The bidding of his name: he lessened pain.
And many already beckoned by Persephone he led
From her cold antechamber home to their hearths again.

GA VII, no. 534; Loeb II, p. 286
Automedon of Aetolia

Friend, cherish your life. Don't put to sea in a bad season
For even with luck, a human being does not last long.
Unlucky Cleonicus, trading in Coelesyria
And hastening home, still trading, to bright Thasos
On that last leg just at the setting of the Pleiades
He went down with them who are called the sailing stars.

GA VI, no. 4; Loeb I, p. 300
Leonidas of Tarentum

His hooks, easily swallowed, his line, his long poles
His jagged trident (Poseidon's weapon), his creels
Cleverly devised for entry and no exit
The pair of oars from his boat. The wicker basket
He lugged his catch home in. This gear
Not being needed by him any more
The fisherman Diophantus offers as he should
To Glaucus, patron of his craft and livelihood.

GA VII, no. 277; Loeb II, p. 152
Callimachus

Shipwrecked stranger, finding your corpse here on the shore
Leontichus built this tomb for you not knowing who you are
And weeping over his own life lived in peril. For he too must
Like the shearwater wander the salt seas and never be at rest.

GA VII, nos. 214 and 216; Loeb II, pp. 120 and 122
Archias and Antipater of Thessalonica
Burial of a beached dolphin

Dolphin, flung up here on sharp rocks high above high tide
We who drag a poor living out of the dangerous sea
Having witnessed your agony and lamenting
The loss of one more of your companionable kind
Who dance in rainbowed water either side our bows
To a music we cannot hear, who obligingly ferry the Nereids
All the far way to the deep pool of Tethys, over you

Leaper and diver, show-off, smiling entertainer
Wiping the warm blood off you, mending you as best we can
Now above the highest high water with the stones that gashed you
Against the rats and the black-backs we raise this tomb
Adding you to our beloved ghosts. Quicken our hearing
Friendly dolphin, let us into your deep-sea conversations
In the time we have left help us teach our children.

III

GA X, no. 5; Loeb IV, p. 4
Thyillus

The swallows are rebuilding their homes of mud
Flowers overflow Persephone's own meadow
Zephyrus soothes the surface of the flood
And the loud strait hushes its mouth. Time to stow
The anchors aboard, coil the hawsers, set free
All your canvas to the beckoning wind. So Priapus
Our grinning harbour-master, counsels us
Whose lives are in the gift of the fickle sea.

GA VII, no. 260; Loeb II, p. 144
Carphyllides

Wayfarer passing by our tomb, think of us in death
As fortunate mortals, content. Man and wife we lived
As one flesh aging together on the good earth and left
Children's children. Girls and boys continued the line
Of our good fortune, we sang them to sleep in our laps
No mortal sickness befalling any one of them, no grief
Befell us. But on this our grave they poured libations
And sent us to sleep among the lucky in love and life.

GA VII, no. 270; Loeb II, p. 148
Simonides

These sailing with the first-fruits to bright Apollo's shrine
Are berthed in darkness everlasting now, deep down.

GA IX, III, no. 314; Loeb III, p. 168

Anyte of Tegea
A statue of Hermes

I, Hermes, stand here by a row of windswept trees
Where three roads meet near the grey shore.
Tired wayfarers, this is a place of ease
And the spring gives water that is cold and clear.

GA VI, no. 170; Loeb I, p. 386

Thyillus

These elms, these tall willows, this wide-spreading plane
And the spring of clear cold water in their shade
Are sacred to Pan. Shepherds, he welcomes you.
Dip the tin cups and drink deep and give him thanks.

GA VII, no. 486; Loeb II, p. 264

Anyte of Tegea

Often she comes here, Cleina, mother to her daughter's tomb
    Mourning her short-lived child, beloved Philaenis, and calling
The soul of her back who, being denied the passage from girl to wife
    Came instead to pale Acheron and there she passed over.

GA VII, no. 507b; Loeb II, p. 276
Simonides

Unwedded, gone to Persephone, like her
Our Callias was a girl with golden hair.

GA VII, no. 271; Loeb II, p. 148
Callimachus

It was the lure of the swift ships killed our son
And all we have here is a tomb that bears his name.
Paterius himself, our softly spoken one
The sea withholds from us who want him home.

GA VII, no. 212; Loeb II, p. 120
Mnasalcas

Stranger, returning home, tell them you saw the tomb
Of wind-footed Aethyia, reared on dry land, lightest of limb
Often with ships keeping pace she ran the long course and always
Like her namesake, the shearwater, went the distance.

GA IX, no. 142; Loeb III, p. 72
Anonymous

Climber on the crags, piper to the Nymphs, horned Pan
We who have come here thirsting entreat you
Let this spring water run as it has always run
Cold and plenteous from a safe pure source deep below.

GA XVI, no. 264 a; Loeb V, p. 316
Anonymous

This statue is sacred to the Nymphs. The well is in their care
So caring may they let its waters flow for ever more.

GA IX, nos. 257 & 258; Loeb III, p. 136
Apollonides and Antiphanes of Megalopolis

This was the spring above all others around here
The Nymphs loved and praised. She ran cold and pure
Sweet on the parched throat, ever abundant, clear
Till a man came and washed his soiled hands in her
And she shrank back into the dark, the Nymphs too
Went elsewhere, the road in horror makes a detour.
Only the very thirsty, hoping against hope, like you
Traveller, still come and kneel for what's not there.

GA IX, no. 374; Loeb III, p. 204
Anonymous

About half-way, friend, on your left at a little distance
There's a grove of plane trees and laurel. Don't miss it. You're
       half way
And nothing like it again. The laurel and plane make a shade
Over a cold clean spring. Drink, have a lie-down, close your eyes

Cover your face with your hat and listen to the water
Let your soul drink deep of her and believe she will live and give
For ever. Miss that place off your road at a little distance
You'll be as good as dead when you get where you have to be.

GA IX, no. 313; Loeb III, p. 168
Anyte of Tegea

Come here under the leafing canopy of the laurel.
Sit by the spring and drink, the water is sweet.
You are tired from labouring in the summer heat.
Rest now, the touch of cooling Zephyrus is gentle.

GA IX, no. 706; Loeb III, p. 388
Antipater of Thessalonica (?)

Do me no harm. I am young, I am a holy tree.
Cut me, I bleed. Bark me, I'll stand for all to see
Dead, like a curse imploring the sky.
Best you believe all trees are holy trees
But the poplar, as everyone knows
Lives in the especial care of the Sun.
Three who were once the sisters of Phaeton
There at the unhealed place where the ash of him lies
Whisper through their countless leaves of a world so dry
It is home to nothing but dead everlasting life
Without water even for the tears of grief.
Listen to me, stranger, human passer-by.

GA VII, no. 199; Loeb II, p. 112
Tymnes
On an unknown bird called Elaeus

He writes of the loss of a bird called Elaeus
The Graces nurtured her and like the halcyon
Singing she made a calm around her in the sea
She had sweet breath, she loved the light of the sun
He mourns the departure of a gentleness that we
Can't even put a name to and no one
Supposes she would have tarried long with us.

GA IX, no. 220; Loeb III, p. 114
Thallus of Miletus

Over the lovers and their mysteries
The green plane tree extends its whispering boughs and these
Are threaded through with an inter-fingering vine and this
Lets down black grapes into easy reach. Allow your devotees
In hiding here a stay of time, Cypris.

GA VI, no. 119; Loeb I, p. 362
Moero of Byzantium

Black cluster full of the juice of Dionysus
Severed and hanging now in the golden porch of Aphrodite
Never again will your mother extend a loving arm for you
And cover your head with a scarf of scented leaves.

GA V, no. 8; Loeb I, p. 132
Meleager

Night and the lamp, we took
None other into the confidence of our vows,
Swearing to love, never to leave,
Calling them to witness. Now
Those promises, he says, were written on water.
The lamp shines on him sleeping elsewhere.

GA V, no. 169; Loeb I, 208
Asclepiades

Sweet in summer to the thirsty is a draught of snow
And sweet to sailors after winter gales are the zephyrs of spring
But when they share their bodies' gifts and honour Cypris doing so
Two lovers under one cloak are the sweetest thing.

GA VI, no. 162; Loeb I, p. 382
Meleager

To you Meleager dedicates this lamp, his playful accomplice
Sharer with him of the secrets of your night-festival, Cypris.

GA VII, no. 181; Loeb II, p. 102
Andronicus

Beloved Democrateia you have gone –
Oh the pity of it! – into the dark house of Acheron
Bequeathing to your mother the ancient grief. You dead
She sharpens steel and cuts the grey locks from her head.

GA VII, no. 649; Loeb II, p. 346
Anyte of Tegea

Beloved and unwedded child of mine
Leaving me childless so we shall remain.
I visit a likeness of you made of stone
And speak what cannot be and might have been.

GA IX, no. 556; Loeb III, p. 308
Zonas

Nymphs of the riverbanks, yesterday you were
My witnesses when he, burnt by the dog-star
Into your cool waters flung himself and washed
The bloom of dust off his fair skin. Tell me this:
Was he not beautiful? The sun had blushed
His apple-cheeks. And am I not a goat
Heart-lamed, hoofed and hairy, limping upright
Through these, the dog-days, for the boy Daphnis?

GA VI, 110; Loeb I, p. 358
Leonidas of Tarentum *or* Mnasalcas

By the coiling Maeander from ambush under the hill
Damis into this stag thrust deep his whetted spear
Hewed off the eight-tined glory of its brow and here
High on this thriving pine nailed it, to boast his kill.

GA VI, no. 153; Loeb I, p. 376
Anyte of Tegea

This cauldron would hold an ox. It is given to Athena
By Cleobotus, son of Eriaspidas, citizen of spacious Tegea.
Its maker is Aristoteles, son of another of that name
And by the Clitorius, whose fishes sing, he is at home.

GA IX, no. 71; Loeb III, p. 36
Antiphilus of Byzantium

This oak tree from on high extends its shade
To those at the mercy of noon on the open road.
It roofs closer than tiles with its leafy boughs
A home for the cicada and the wood pigeon.
Human and fugitive from the killing sun
I want that dark light kinder on the eyes.

GA VI, no. 177; Loeb I, p. 388
Anonymous

White-skinned Daphnis, player of pretty airs
Dedicates to Pan the dappled fawn's skin
The pierced pipes, this sharp spear, the stick for killing hares
And the leather bag he carried apples in.

GA VI, no. 73; Loeb I, p. 338
Macedonius the Consul

I, Daphnis the piper, now a trembling old man
And my hands no good for work, dedicate to Pan
Who loves the wild places my shepherd's crook.

I give up my labours and my woolly flock
But still I play the pipes and the voice that houses
In my shaking body is true and steady still.

The wolves on the mountains are ravenous.

Unaging Pan, who taught me, let no new pupil
No new beloved piper to your goats, go tell
The howling wolves how feeble your Daphnis is.

GA IX, no. 401; Loeb III, p. 222
Palladas of Alexandria

Nature loving the rules that bind true friends
Invented means to help in the state of absence.
Pen, paper, ink, our handwriting. Love sends
Signals by these, pining in the distance.

GA IX, no. 88; Loeb III, p. 46
Philippus of Thessalonica

They get blown off course, the singletons, they fall
As foreigners in some unwelcoming place
But one, a nightingale, cursing the wind of Thrace
From where no good had come to her, so small
Between the black sky and the unending sea
Failing, falling, her long trajectory
Was well judged by a dolphin. He met its point of entry
And days and nights then was her trusted ferryman.
She, close at his ear, above his smile, paid him his due
Of thanks with singing. But dolphins quite often
As lovers of music, singers themselves in the deep blue
Have served the Muses, after human savagery
Arion, like Philomela, ferrying to safety.

GA V, no. 156; Loeb I, p. 202
Meleager

I washed up here because her clear blue eyes
Gave me the certain promise of calm seas.

GA VII, no. 510; Loeb II, p. 276
Simonides

Death intercepted you, Cleisthenes
Wandering the sea that we call kind to strangers.
Dust and earth of its foreign shore obscure your face.
Who wants you home in Chios wants in vain.

GA XI, no. 8; Loeb IV, p. 70
Anonymous

You only waste your garlands and the myrrh
On tombstones; do not feed the pyre.
Bestow your gifts upon me living if you would.
Wine on my ashes now makes only mud.

GA V, no. 11; Loeb, I, p. 132
Anonymous

Goddess, beloved Cypris, saviour of men at sea
I'm one shipwrecked and lost on land, save me.

GA V, no. 17; Loeb I, p. 136
Gaetulicus

Guardian of the surf-beaten shore, I send you
These little cakes and simple gifts of sacrifice.
For tomorrow I shall cross the wide Ionian Sea
Hurrying into the arms of my Idothea.
Shine favourably on my love and on my ship
Queen of our bed, Cypris, as of the shore.

IV

GA X, no. 4; Loeb IV, p. 4
Marcus Argentarius

Loose the stern-cables from your moored-up boat
Hoist your reluctant sails, trader, and put out.
Seems the storms are done. Softly Zephyrus
Lends the blue-grey waves a girl's gentleness.
Churring, twittering, swallows are building
Clay and straw chamber-homes for desired offspring.
Listen then to Priapus who bids you begin
The unremitting business of the sea again.

GA V, no. 190; Loeb I, p. 222
Meleager

Salt wave of love, unsleeping gales of jealousy
A whole winter sea of song and wine, I have let go
The rudder of my judgement. Where am I carried to?
Beyond my Scylla's kisses eternally.

GA VII, no. 497; Loeb II, p. 270
Damagetus

Here now another father with lost hopes has come
And builds among several another waiting tomb.
He supposes his son is lying without rites somewhere
Unsheltered, not even gathered, his bones picked bare
Strewn far away, on Euxeinus' long inhospitable shore
And builds him an empty house and wishes him home.

GA V, no. 199; Loeb I, p. 226
Hedylus

The wine, going often between us,
Laid me to sleep at the mercy of his love.
What was put off I lay before you, Cypris,
My girlhood in the clothes sodden with perfume.

GA VII, nos. 163 and 164; Loeb II, p. 92
After Leonidas of Tarentum and Antipater of Sidon

Who are you, lady, lying below this Parian marble?
    Praxo, child of Calliteles. – Your country? – Samos.
Who laid you to rest here? – Theocritus, whose wife I was.
    How did you die? – In childbirth. – And how old? – Twenty-two.
And having no children? – I left behind me Calliteles
    My three-year-old son. – May he live for you, lady
And his grey head be blessed in his old age. – And you, traveller
    May the paths be kind and bring you where you belong.

GA V, no. 235; Loeb I, p. 246
Macedonius the Consul

I had small hope or none but you, longed for, are here
And by this wonder shake me free of bad imagining
The vessel of me breaks with much unpent desire
My small soul in love's risen sea is drowning.
This shipwreck near dry land appearing, save him
And into your safe harbour, love, receive him.

GA V, no. 175; Loeb I, p. 212
Meleager

I know that crossing your heart you lie, your hair
Is damp with new scents and says so, your eyes
Black for want of sleep, the garland likewise
Slant, falling off your head, they say what you are.
Who tousled your curls, who plied you with wine, neat?
You can't walk straight and you're not talking right.
You're everyone else's, not mine. The plucked string,
The mad castanets are calling you back where you belong.

GA IX, no. 315; Loeb III, p. 170
Nicias

Weary as you are, sit here beneath these poplars, wayfarer
Come close, drink deep of our fountain and when
You are distant, remember it. For here a father
Simus, stands in effigy close to Gillus, his dead son

GA VII, no. 646; Loeb II, p. 344
Anyte of Tegea

Erato then still holding him in her embrace
And wetting her cheeks and his with her fresh tears
Spoke her last words: Oh, father, I am no longer yours
With his black shadow Death has already veiled my face.

GA IX, no. 326; Loeb III, p. 176
Leonidas of Tarentum

Nymphs of this spring that leaps from the cloven rock
I leave you, among your many small wooden likenesses
That rough hands carved and the splashing forever freshens,
This cup I dipped deep in your water. Allow the next
Who comes here thirsty the use of it. Be with me, Nymphs
Murmur of your cold springs as I slog on under the sun.

GA IX, no. 745; Loeb III, p. 404
Anyte of Tegea

Rowdy Dionysus' friend, this goat, in a pool in the mountains
Stands admiring the long soft fork of his shaggy beard.
Often through his reflection the Naiad of the place has risen
Smiling and around her rosy finger has twisted his curls.

GA XVI, no. 17; Loeb V, p. 168
Anonymous

O Pan, run your grinning lips along the golden reeds
Play a holy tune to my she-goats while they pasture
Give them another day's good herbage so I'll be sure
Of the gift of the white and frothing milk our living needs.
Do this and at your altar their lord will stand and spew
The red blood from his shaggy breast for you.

GA XVI, no. 254; Loeb V, p. 310
Anonymous

You passers-by along this highway who
Stone by stone have raised me, Hermes, a sacred pile
For that small kindness no big thanks: I tell you
To Goat Fountain it is another mile

GA VII, no. 736; Loeb II, p. 390
Leonidas of Tarentum

Chin up, friend, dragging your life, old rolling stone
From one place to another and never your own
Come dusk, out of the way maybe you'll spot a shack
No one else on the high road and you duck in quick

And maybe there's a grate and the makings of a fire
And you've still got the pitta that woman at her door
Bestowed, smiling, her olives, her sprig of mint and thyme
And your stoppered bottle she filled with the black-red wine.

Wayfarer god, give him a good night's sleep, keep him warm
He'll be gone by daybreak, he'll have done no harm.

GA IX, no. 327; Loeb III, p. 176
Hermocreon

Nymphs of these springs, I thirsting, footsore
Lighting upon your home in this saving place
Thanks is my only offering and a prayer the waters here
And the dancing of your white feet will never cease

GA XVI, no. 256; Loeb V, p. 312
Anonymous
A statue of Hermes

Traveller, this place I live in is a hilly wilderness
And not my choice or fault, Archelochus put me here
I, Hermes, am not at home on a mountain, sir
A busy road is my idea of happiness
Something going on, a bit of conversation, that's my scene
But Archelochus loves solitude and wants no nextdoor neighbour
So he's only got me and I've only got him for company
Week in, week out never a mortal soul goes by
And when anyone does they're more his sort than mine.

GA VI, no. 199; Loeb I, p. 400
Antiphilus of Byzantium

Antiphilus dedicates his hat, sign of the wayfarer, to you
Hecate, goddess of the crossroads, who
Heeded his prayers and blessed the ways he went.
Small offering but devoutly meant.
And let no passer-by lay hands on it. Theft here
Even of a small thing, will cost the thief dear.

GA XVI, no. 258; Loeb V, p. 312

Anonymous

The Cretan stood me, Pan, as you see me, by the holy fire
In Dictynna's shrine in bronze with the hooves of a goat.
I wear a skin and hold two hare-staves and high up here
From my cave in the rock towards the hill keep a sharp look-out.

GA XVI, no. 291; Loeb V, p. 334

Anyte of Tegea

Theodotus the shepherd set this gift here under the hill
For tousle-headed Pan and the nymphs of the fold
Because he was parched and wearied by the summer heat until
Cupping their hands, they offered him water, sweet and cold.

GA IX, no. 298; Loeb III, p. 160

Antiphilus of Byzantium

They speak of one who got from Athens to Eleusis
With the help of his stick and strangers along the way.
He was as blind to the sunlit world as to the Mysteries.
But in that night Demeter opened wide his eyes
And through them lit his soul as bright as day.
He left his stick at her shrine. Home then, what none
May speak of they saw shining in his vision.

GA VII, no. 272; Loeb II, p. 148
Callimachus

Lycus of Naxos did not die on land but lost
His ship, his livelihood and his life at sea
When he put out from Aegina, to trade.
Now he and his home are severed eternally.
He feeds the fish and obeys the wind and tide.
His tomb here says when the Kids set dry land's best.

GA IX, no. 329; Loeb III, p. 178
Leonidas of Tarentum

Nymphs of this spring, diligently water Timocles' garden
For he never fails to give you its gifts as they come into season.

GA XVI, no. 228; Loeb V, p. 294
Anyte of Tegea

Midsummer in the leaves there's a murmuring breath of air.
Among the roots a cold spring bubbles through.
Wayfarer, weary to death, here is kindness to spare.
Earthly, heavenly, as the tree lives, so may you.

GA VI, no. 238; Loeb I, p. 426
Apollonidas

I, Euphron, an old man, remind you, god of round here
That I plough a patch so hard and dry the share
Only scratches the surface and my total furrows are few.
Vines no good either, wine not enough to see me through.
Of this little, little will come your way. But give me more
Of my plenty you'll be served first and get plenty too.

GA IX, no. 21; Loeb III, p. 12
Anonymous

Thessaly, breeder of horses, you named me Pegasus
And I was led victorious in the procession at Pytho
And on the Isthmus and at the festival of Zeus
At Nemea, and in Arcadia I was crowned
With the plaited olive. Homeland, tell me now
Is it right, is it kind of you, that I must turn and turn
This deadweight stone of Nisyros and grind
Fine for you Demeter's gifts of the ears of corn
I in old age, after my many victories, whom you
When my mother had licked me clean named Pegasus?

GA VII, no. 215; Loeb II, p. 122
Anyte of Tegea

She flung up here on the dirty tideline, those
Are bloody holes that were her eyes
And that encrusted spattering of white is where
The gulls perched hacking at them and the rest of her.

Another subtracted from the cheerful company
Of creatures who seemed once to love humanity
And surfaced, smiling, snorting, leaped and played
Around our prows that once were dolphin-eyed.

With them, warm blood in common, we had access
To the ancient depths. The loss, the loss!
She lies now stranded under the sun and moon
Eyeless, ripped to the bone, not fit to be seen

Among our trash that will live for ever.
Come soon, spring tide, recover what's left of her.

GA VII, no. 176; Loeb II, p. 100
Antiphilus of Byzantium

Not because dead I lacked due rights do I lie here
A naked corpse on the corn-bearing earth. Ah no:
Piously by loved ones I was housed below
And am evicted now by the ploughman's iron share.
They say death delivers us from all ills but I
Am shown like carrion to the ever-hungry sky.

GA VII, 268; Loeb II, p. 146
Plato

I whom you look upon here am a shipwrecked man.
The sea took pity and refrained from stripping me bare.
It was a man with shameless hands who went that far.
For so great a wrongdoing so small a gain.
Let him be wearing it when his life too is done
And he stands before Minos in that ragged cloak of mine.

GA VII, no. 157; Loeb II, p. 88
Anonymous

Seems fixed in the heavens my lot of life shall be
Three decades and a three. Well, that will do for me.
Sooner go down in the glorious bloom of life than last
Till ninety-nine like Nestor forever bleating of times past.

GA VII, no. 295; Loeb II, p. 160
Leonidas of Tarentum

Old man Theris who lived on the luck of his pots
Rowed a small caïque, at times raised a scrap of red sail
Lifted fish, dragged a net, rummaged in the rock-holes
Longer seafaring than the shearwaters and neither
The gales when Arcturus sets nor a hurricane
Put a stop to the decades of his life, on the beach
He died, in his hut of reeds, of his own accord
In the great sum of his years, like a lamp going out.
This mound's not raised for him by his wife and children
But by the fraternity of fishermen, his mates.

GA VII, 300; Loeb II, p. 162
Simonides

Earth covers here two brothers from whom life
Withheld the best. Their father, Megaristus, set
This monument to them believing in his grief
That it will last a while as they did not.

GA VII, 341; Loeb II, p. 184
Proclus

I Proclus of Lycia was fostered by Syrianus
To be his successor in the School. This tomb
Now having received the bodies of both of us
I wish our souls might likewise share one home.

GA VII, 359; Loeb II, p. 192
Anonymous

Had you found me dead and buried me for pity
For that good work the gods would have rewarded you
But you my murderer who buried me to hide me
May what you did to me be done to you.

GA VII, no. 378; Loeb II, p. 202
Apollonides

Diotimus dying, within the hour
His wife Erato followed him. Those two then as in life
Lay in one room, under one roof, and were
A solace and a wonder to the living in their love and grief.

GA VII, no. 174; Loeb II, p. 98

Erycias

You are done playing pastoral tunes under this tall plane
Therimachus. Done are the days
When in the shade of this oak you lolled at your ease
And breathed a sweet music to life through your reed
And the cattle stood still and listened and lowed.
Their herdsman, their maker of music, silenced by fire from heaven
At night-fall the cattle came hastily down
To the byre, the slant snow driving them in.

GA VII, nos. 8 and 9; Loeb II, pp. 6 and 8

After Antipater of Sidon and Damagetus
The death of Orpheus, son of Calliope

You dead, we have nobody now for a go-between, none
The shy forest animals will trust and come to for music
We shall not see them close and enchanted ever again
Nor will the oaks quietly uproot and like small children
Form a circle around the lyre's soft-spoken centre.
The inner life of rocks, the dance of their atoms, is lost to us
And hark at the winds, already deafening, hail will smash
Our efforts at nurture, snow settle in deep, and the sea

Tide after tide will be higher than our houses, the elements
Have turned vengeful, they have lost a dear friend, they assume
We killed you. The closest, most necessary, immortals
Let you into their secrets, they watched and listened
With pleasure and with admiration while you fashioned
Verse in our mother tongue into native metres
The better to be got by heart. The links are undoing
Already very few of us remember how they fit.

GA XVI, no. 231; Loeb V, p. 296
Anyte of Tegea

Why, Pan of the fields, do you sit here to play
In this deep shade, in the heart of a wood, at break of day?

Because my music travels and the beasts men own are curious.
In sleep they will hear what their owners have forfeited
And will step out at dewfall and come dreaming towards my music
Across the silver-grey mountain in the chilly sunlight
Through beautiful wet tresses of wild oats. Invisible
I will draw them from the four quarters
I will encourage the heart-of-hearts in each of them
They will halt in a musing circle around this wood
And attend to my music coming out of its darkness
My gift to them, their gift to me, their listening, in them and in me
Fealty to the spheres' eternal music will be rewarded.

Alcaeus of Messene

Time was, traveller, in these parts towards noon
If you'd kept still you might have heard Pan play.
Yes, Pan, the walker on the mountains before he slept
He'd lift the syrinx to his lips and across
The empty pipes he breathed and the breath would bring
To life the longing for water in our parched land
And cause the springs of song to start up again deep down
And marrying then his music to that singing
And striking the beat and the rhythm they required
He beckoned the Nymphs who feel through their white feet
The melodies of the waters that thrive underground
Whatever our drought above, he breathed them up
With all their stored knowledge. Not so very long ago
You might have known as we did the tread of the Nymphs
And how they wreathed their singing around the sly
Goat-footed, horned and bearded Pan who knows what lives
In each of his thirteen syrinx-reeds, in waiting. This
The breathing, the singing, the white feet of the Nymphs
Foot-farer through our country, you might have witnessed
Until he ceased and in the shade like a forlorn child
Still clutching his pipes, he slept. The dancers vanished
But for a while in the heat of noon you might have heard
As we think he did in his dreams, the revels lingering
Stranger, passer-by. I pray to Pan and the Nymphs
That you will live henceforth in your elsewhere haunted
And won't forget us and our vanished local streams.

GA IX, no. 242; Loeb III, p. 126
Antiphilus of Byzantium

Born and bred on the shores of Thasos, forever
Ferrying folk to and fro between island and mainland
Sure ploughman of the sea, if he dozed at the tiller
Still his boat held her course. She's friends with the wind
Trust her, he said, trust me. Towards the end
Old beyond reckoning, he had the look
Of something barnacled stuck fast on a wreck
And wouldn't be parted. Her and me, he said, me and her.
Upturn her over me and light her for my pyre.
So they sailed to Hades together, faithful pair.

V

GA X, no. 6; Loeb IV, p. 6
Satyrus

Zephyrus, begetter of grass, now moistens
The meadows into flower with his breath.
The arriving swallows swap stories of life and death.
In the warmer sun the sea smiles and quietens.
Go then, take heart, cast off the cables, spread
Wide the wings of your sails. Priapus, god
Of the waterfront, ushers us out to trade
The little we can spare for the much we need.

GA VII, 710; Loeb II, p. 376
Erinna

Erinna carved these words on my white stone to tell
Locals or citizens of elsewhere passing by
That my father named me Baucis and Tenos was
My home. Erinna hears the grief the Sirens sing
For her sweet friend gone below out of earshot now
And all this cold tomb holds is my small yield of ash.

GA VII, no. 273; Loeb II, p. 148
Leonidas of Tarentum

It was the sudden squall of a south-easterly
And night and the black waves of Orion
At his setting sank me. Don't believe my stone.
I slid from life at the centre of the Libyan sea
And turn now on a wheel of water, fed upon.
I, Tharsys, am dispersing, bone by bone.

GA VII, no. 175; Loeb II, p. 100
Antiphilus of Byzantium

So the market's good? You want more land to plough.
Your oxen trudge across ridges of tombs and through
The tenants' ashes drag the share. What will this yield?
What will you make on this invaded field?
There'll come a time when you and yours will die
And want remembering kindly where you lie.

GA VII, no. 185; Loeb, p. 104
Antipater of Thessalonica

The Italian earth holds me, an African.
I lie here where the Tiber meets the sea.
As though I were her daughter Pompeia wept for me
And buried me in the grave of a free woman.
The torch she wished to light my marriage bed
Lit me the way to Persephone instead.

GA VII, no. 246; Loeb II, p. 138
After Antipater of Sidon

Choking the little river we made a bridge that he
Softly could ride across. In time we countless
Were nudged along below the town of Issus
To dispersal in the everlasting and voracious sea.

GA VII, no. 246 a; Loeb II, p. 138
Anonymous

In the manoeuvring for where best to stand and fight
Alexander abandoned Issus and his sick and wounded there.
Darius, entering without opposition, cut off their hands.
Come spring and the melt, will our streams run cold and clear?

GA VII, nos. 256 and 259; Loeb II, pp. 142, 144
Plato

They killed our men and we the women and children
Lie dead near Susa now not having seen again
Eretria our beloved city nor listened ever again
In house and home in our sleep to the close Aegean.

GA VI, no. 228; Loeb I, p. 420
Addaeus of Macedon

When his labouring ox was worn out by old age and the furrows
Alcon, reverencing him for his service, led him not to the slaughter
But to a meadow of deep grass. There how this fellow creature
When Alcon strolls out to visit him at the hour of shadows
In grateful delight lifts up his head and bellows!

GA VII, no. 202; Loeb II, p. 114
Anyte of Tegea

You my dawn-caller I could not wake without
Oh my red and golden herald, my chanticleer
Now the fox while you were sleeping has ripped your throat
I wake in the silence, in your absence, at your hour.

GA VII, no. 254 a; Loeb II, p. 142
Simonides

Timolytus, of Gortys, here in the earth I lie
Who came to trade and get a living, not to die.

GA VII, no. 274; Loeb II, p. 150
Honestus of Byzantium

I call the name of Timocles and scan
The bitter sea for the corpse of him and know
Grief on a stone will not haul in a man
Who fed the ravenous fishes long ago.

GA VII, no. 280; Loeb II, p. 152
Isidorus of Aegae

This hillock is a grave. Ploughman, leave it be.
On your land it is a holding of the gods below
Watched over night and day by the immortal sky.
So let it flower for loss and may your yield be great.

GA VII, no. 211; Loeb II, p. 118
Tymnes

This stone announces it holds here below
The white Maltese, in life Bull was his name
Eumelus' faithful guardian. But call him now
Lost in the silent dark he can't come home.

GA VII, no. 281; Loeb II, p. 154
Heraclides

Swerve the oxen, ploughman, lift the share.
A nameless fellow-mortal lies buried here
A stranger, a hungry man, a traveller footsore
Who says to you: Friend, I am in your care.

GA VII, no. 285; Loeb II, p. 154
Glaucus of Nicopolis

Not this earth and this slight stone but all out there
All that visible sea lies upon Cleodemus.
For he went down with his ship and where his white bones are
Ask the shearwaters. They know if anyone does.

GA VII, no. 292; Loeb II, p. 158
Theon of Alexandria

Somewhere the halcyons may care for you, Lenaeus.
Here day after day your mother tends an emptiness.

GA VII, no. 228; Loeb II, p. 128

Anonymous

Androtion built me for himself and his wife and children
But I am not yet a tomb for anyone
And long may I so remain but when I must
Receive them may the earliest be first and the latest last.

GA VII, no. 477; Loeb II, p. 260

Tymnes

Don't let it weigh on your heart, Philaenis
That you are not lying beside the Nile but here
At Eleutherna. From wherever you are
Your one and only road is the road to Hades.

GA VII, no. 500; Loeb II, p. 272

Asclepiades

Wayfarer passing by my empty tomb
Should you come to Chios tell my father Architeles
That a bad south-easter sank me and my merchandise.
Of his son Euippus nothing is left but the name.

GA VII, no. 505; Loeb II, p. 274

Sappho

On Pelagon's grave his father Meniscus places oar and pot:
With these he sought the livelihood he never got.

GA VII, 265; Loeb II, p. 146
Plato

I, a sailor, lie here. He, a ploughman, lies over there.
On land, at sea, Death stalks the living everywhere.

GA VII, no. 537; Loeb II, p. 288
Phanias

Not for his father but for his lost son
Did Lysis grieving build this empty tomb
Solemnly burying the name of him, Saon
Since nothing else will be delivered home.

GA VII, no. 631; Loeb II, 338
Apollonides

Should you come to Apollo's harbour at Miletus
Tell Diogenes the bad news: his son
Philo, shipwrecked, lies in the earth of Andros
Having drunk deep of the waters of the Aegean.

GA VII, 582; Loeb II, p. 312
Julianus, Prefect of Egypt

Greetings, mariner crossing to Hades, curse the sea
If you will, that drowned you but be glad
Of the small mercy of the winds for they
Rolled you ashore close to the tombs of your fathers.

GA VII, no. 569; Loeb II, p. 306
Agathias Scholasticus

Yes, traveller, when you see my homeland Thessaly
I beg you, tell my beloved husband that she
Who was his wife is dead and lies in a tomb
Alas in the earth hard by the Bosporus shore
But wishes he will build her a cenotaph close to home
So she will be remembered who is not there.

GA VII, no. 637; Loeb II, 340
Antipater of Thessalonica

Pyrrhus, solo oarsman, from his little boat
Going for small fry with a hair line
Far from land was struck by a thunderbolt.
A calm day, no mortal but him in sight.
Very slowly the soft tide brought him ashore
Blackened, smouldering, stinking of sulphur.
Pyrrhus who went far out and fished alone.

GA VII, no. 642; Loeb II, 342
Apollonides

Between Syros and Delos the sea took
Theris of Samos. His father sick,
He was hastening home by the sun and the stars.
So much the sea cares for our love and fears.

GA VII, 739; Loeb II, p. 392
Phaedimus

Here the young wife Aristagora housed the dust
Of her young husband Antheus
Whom the savage Aegean drowned off Skiathos.
A fisherman caught him drifting deep among the lost
Hauled him alongside and roping his ankles tight
Towed him to harbour in Torone at first light.
Stranger, visitor, think of them all three:
The dust, the widow and that good charioteer of the sea.

GA VII, 744; Loeb II, p. 394
Diogenes Laertius

They say the astronomer Eudoxus, teaching in Memphis
The eternal lives of the spheres, learned his own fate from Apis
The young bull who between his golden horns bore the full moon.
Not that Nature suddenly gave this beast the power to speak
But standing sideways-on, he put out his feeling tongue
And licked and licked at the travelling scholar's cloak.
Which was his way of telling him, Thinker, you are on the wane.
Lover of the earth and the heavens, you don't have long.

GA XVI, no. 229; Loeb V, 296
Anonymous

Out of Zeus himself our dearest sprang and the cloud you see
Around his head is proof of it. For Zeus, Cloud-Gatherer
On the mountain goddess Maia fathered Hermes, the Wayfarer
Who fathered the goatherd Pan on the tree-nymph Dryope.

GA VII, no. 724; Loeb II, p. 384
Anyte of Tegea

Fighting, your courage killed you. At home before long
Your death in black mourning draped the house room after room.
On the white stone above you, what comfort the beautiful song
That you, son, husband, father, died fighting for house and home?

GA VII, no. 721; Loeb II, p. 382
Chaeremon

So we engaged, being equal with them in men and weaponry.
The prize for us or them was another people's city.
We there only for that gave up all hope of returning home.
We left it to the carrion birds to report the foul outcome.

GA VII, no. 723; Loeb II, p. 384
Anonymous

Smoke wreathes your lovely river. Your trees are felled.
You'll want for shade. Where shall the sweet birds build?
The wolves are shepherding in your sheep. All hard to bear
These things not having been done to you before.

GA VI, 189; Loeb I, p. 396
Moero of Byzantium

Daughters of Anigrus, whose healing streams you paddle in
Immortal nymphs of this place, for you Architeles
Has set up under your pines these wooden images
Clean as he could make them and begs you cure his skin.

GA VII, no. 535; Loeb II, p. 288
Meleager

Pan, losing the boy Daphnis, will come,
He says, into the town with his grief.
Because Daphnis is dead the herds will want a master,
The mountains music and the wild animals a hunter.
The god Pan will be among townspeople,
Goat-footed, lamentable.

GA VI, 113; Loeb I, p. 360
Simmias Grammaticus

In a former time I was the curving pair
Of horns on a wild goat such as climb high
On the rocky cliffs, my curly hair
Often garlanded with greenery. Now by
The hands of a master turner I am joined
And smoothed into a bow for Nicomachus
Strung with the sinew of an ox and thus
Given him for battle, strong and finely tuned.

GA XVI, no. 126; Loeb V, p. 230
Anonymous
The Minotaur

This is the bull child, the nothing complete
The man half beast, a double kind
His mother's yen in broad daylight
Bull head, man trunk, the errant joined
It is the waking living dream
That can't be sent back whence it came.

GA VII, no. 653; Loeb II, p. 348
Pancrates

Sirocco, raising the Aegean, sank Epierides.
He went down in the setting of the Hyades
Himself, his ship, his crew. His father Cimon
Has built this empty tomb for one dead son.

GA VII, no. 155; Loeb II, p. 88
Anonymous
On Philistion the Comic of Nicaea

I, Philistion of Nicaea, the Comic, who into the gruel
Of human misery mixed laughter, many times I died
But now in these lendings of the many parts I played
Of too much laughing lie here, curtains, dead for real.

GA VII, no. 660; Loeb II, p. 352
Leonidas of Tarentum

I, Orthon of Syracuse, advise you, passer-by
Do not go wandering drunk in a winter night.
I'd have a roomy tomb at home but somehow I
Ended up here in foreign soil curled up tight.

GA X, no. 17; Loeb IV, p. 12
Antiphilus

God of the seed and spawn, Priapus, ease
The departing sails of the poet Demodocus
Through quiet water with a gentle breeze
Into the open sea. And you, Cypris
Lady of the headland, be with him whose verses
Owe their life to you and who wakes and prays
A fair west wind will bring him in time to Cos
Sanctuary of the healing god Asclepius.

GA X, no. 17 a; Loeb IV, p. 14

Anonymous

Our soothsayers mumble nothing we don't know.
The swallows are fewer and some arriving die.
Singles repair the homes of a year ago.
Piteous their hope. Our priests look no one in the eye.
All see the signs and none know what they mean.
It is Persephone's advent but we hear of meadows
That are not fit to be seen by the sun or moon.
Zephyrus falters, the slant hail blows.
We know it is time to weigh anchor again
Loose the hawsers, open the sails. But look there:
Another eyeless dolphin has washed in.
Can it be that everywhere is much like here?

CODA

SOME QUATRAINS FOR A PRIMER OF OUR TIMES
(supply your own pictures)

Laws of war

We too had laws of war: don't poison wells
Don't fell the olive trees (they take so long to grow)
Don't bomb the schools, don't bomb the hospitals ...
Stranger seeking our monument, look around you.

Debris

We don't see all you do but quite a lot.
24/7 if we choose. Faster than Ariel
Your deeds girdle the earth. Debris of ill
And some can live with it and some can not.

Behind the eyes

Not being speakable it fled for sanctuary
Behind his eyes and there looks out. What he can't say
This child will harbour in him night and day
And lids tight shut or open wide will always see.

Epitaph

We pile here in the usual ratio
Of us to you. So numerous in death
None has a stone and script to lie beneath.
This cicatrice, this bulldozed trench must do.

Fact

The fact is, friend, we matter more than you.
One husband, lover, son, father of ours
Outweighs at least a hundred such of yours.
It's a fact of life, my friend – and of death too.

Birth pangs

The school fell on her and she came out blind.
Her teacher's in there brained, but never mind:
You don't need brains to know or eyes to see
These are the birth pangs of democracy.

A man in white

Cross or crescent, his calling is to heal
Without frontiers. He is a man in white
And has come out from his blackened hospital
To face more soiled white bags unearthed in daylight.

House and home

In that land now, if let, if possible
They seek what's left of house and home and crawl
Like cavers, muffled, through the chokes of rubble
For proofs of broken life however small.

Child

After. Over and done with. All gone.
She is too small to be left on the road alone.
Another day, another night, will nobody come?
Death will, a kindness, and take her home.

SPIRALS

Spirals

Ammonite and galaxy and all the coils between
For the making line there's no extinction
What you will be is not what you have been
The tip, the growing point, reaches on and on ...

Tower

The shell of one, still roofed but stripped
Except for a handrail round the inside wall
No stairs, only the wooden rail they gripped
Climbing the spiral to their bed. That's all.

The making

Blizzard of swimmers, the launched three hundred million
Charge of the long heads with the furious tails
Through a deep seascape, amid colossal dying, one
Will seed the dream of openings, tunnels, delicate tentacles.

Evolution

This time-lapse you-tube of your earliest embryo days
(The days of gill-slits) shows you how
From where they were on the sides of your head your eyes
Come round to where they are and look best now.

And that groove on your upper lip we call the philtrum
Is where your face's three parts, drifting, met.
So it's a human being you've become:
Might staying fish have been a friendlier lot?

The double helix

The spiral-ladder of the makings of a creature
Its very self, snowflake-unique, the sole and twain
The entwining wreathing wedded signature
Riding the blood's white coracles, thine and mine...

Albatross chick

Opened, this babe's full stomach looks like a trove
Of bright things stowed away for an after-life.
What we cast on the waters is not the food of love.
Nothing will come of us for you but grief.

Ghost-gear

Ghost-gear drifts. Nobody owns it now
Who owned it last lost it or set it free
To float a while under the sun and drift below
And live for ever where it doesn't belong to be

And graceful creatures who are local there
Materialise in it and can't get free
But tangle more. They hang in the ghost-gear
Drift and struggle and will not die quickly.

Nurdles

Nurdles, also known as mermaids' tears
Are little beads we made some time ago
And they will last at least a thousand years
And pass through many guts in doing so.

The dead centre

Here's the still centre and around it wheel
Clockwise the gyres, the vast collectors
Unstoppably, eternally they trawl
The frontiers of sweet and salt, our shores

And river mouths year after year
Like clockwork ferrying the haul
Closer and closer until corralled here
Dead centre, little by little it will fall

Year upon year, down, down, to where
In the darkness under the dead still heart
Creatures come foraging since it's there
The ladders of our nourishment start.

Anthropocene

But one thin layer of us is fired and painted clay.
Try kicking the clods when the slant of the sun is right
Under the olives on a breezy day
Fragments of love and dance still come to light.

Old brace and bit

Preacher Irvine's once, but he lost heart. Myself, I like
Pressing with the left hand, turning with the right
To see rise from a clamped old batten the helix-wake
Of fragrant pristine shavings into the light.

The spheres

I learn (late in the day) their music went unheard
Only the attuned could even imagine it
A various harmony, in movement, chorused, shared
Joy of belonging parts that know they fit.

Orbitings

Does the junk for ever haloing our globe
Move silently or with a whispering curse?
I suppose it flashes like a disco-strobe
And whispers: more and more and worse and worse and worse.

Gliders

Ascending very quietly on the thermals
Quitting them to descend on your own quiet ways
In us on the noisy earth who watch the spirals
Tracing the silence, an old sorrow clarifies.

The waters

Dear waters, so various, so never still
I woke remembering your little vortices
Eddies, tourbillons, idlings below the waterfall
Your gift of backtracking, of allowances
Against the unstoppable direction of travel.

NOTE

Most of the preceding poems, the two parts of the Coda, have already been published elsewhere: four poems from 'Quatrains for a Primer of our Times in *Nine Fathom Deep* (Bloodaxe Books, 2009), and 'Spirals' in *The North*, 69, (2021). They appear again here, with a few additions, because I would not have written them but for my decades of close reading of *The Greek Anthology*. These poems now, in their concerns and in their form, derive from that boundless ancient source. 'Some Quatrains...' is an offspring of Brecht's *War Primer*. Appropriate pictures will perforce come to mind in abundance. 'Spirals' mostly treats life in the Anthropocene: that is to say the harm (becoming irreversible) we do to the other lives we share the planet with.

DC